Harvesttime

Oranges

By Inez Snyder

Welcome Books™

Children's Press®
A Division of Scholastic Inc.
New York / Toronto / London / Auckland / Sydney
Mexico City / New Delhi / Hong Kong
Danbury, Connecticut

Photo Credits: Cover, p. 9 © Ed Young/Corbis; p. 5 © Jacqui Hurst/Corbis; p. 7 © Roger Wood/Corbis; p. 11 © Michael Rose; Frank Lane Picture Agency/Corbis; p. 13 © Charles O'Rear/Corbis; p. 15 © Jonathan Blair/Corbis; p. 17 © Lance Nelson/Corbis; p. 19 © Jeff Albertson/Corbis; p. 21 © Bob Krist/Corbis

Contributing Editors: Shira Laskin and Jennifer Silate
Book Design: Erica Clendening

Library of Congress Cataloging-in-Publication Data

Snyder, Inez.
    Oranges / by Inez Snyder.
    p. cm.—(Harvesttime)
    Includes index.
    Summary: Introduces the orange, from the time it begins to grow from a
    seed until it is sold in a farmer's market.
    ISBN 0-516-27593-3 (lib. bdg.)—ISBN 0-516-25913-X (pbk.)
    1. Oranges—Juvenile literature. 2. Oranges—Harvesting—Juvenile
    literature. [1. Oranges. 2. Harvesting.] I. Title. II. Series.

SB370.O7S69 2004
634'.31—dc22
                                                            2003011999

Contents

Oranges grow from **seeds**.

The seeds are planted in the ground.

5

The seeds grow into trees.

Oranges grow on the trees.

7

A group of orange trees is called a **grove**.

9

First, the oranges are green.

11

Oranges are ready to be **harvested** when they turn orange.

It is warm outside at **harvesttime**.

13

People must **climb** ladders
to pick the oranges.

They put the oranges
into bags.

Then, the oranges are put into tubs.

17

A **machine** picks up the tubs.

The machine drops the oranges into a truck.

The oranges are taken to markets to be sold.

Many people like oranges!

21

New Words

climb (**klime**) to move up something using
 your hands and feet
grove (**grohv**) a group of trees growing or
 planted near one another
harvested (**hahr**-vuhst-ed) picked or gathered
harvesttime (**hahr**-vuhst-time) the season
 when fruits and vegetables become ripe and
 are picked or gathered
machine (muh-**sheen**) something that is made
 to do work or to help make other things
seeds (**seedz**) the parts of plants that can
 grow in soil and make new plants

To Find Out More

Books
Orange Juice
by Betsey Chessen and Pamela Chanko
Scholastic Inc.

Oranges
by Jason Cooper
Rourke Publishing

Web Site
Texas Citrus Cowboy's Kid's Club
http://www.texasweet.com/kids/
Learn about how oranges are harvested and play games
on this Web site.

Index

About the Author
Inez Snyder has written several books to help children learn to read. She also enjoys cooking for her family.

Reading Consultants
Kris Flynn, Coordinator, Small School District Literacy, The San Diego County Office of Education

Shelly Forys, Certified Reading Recovery Specialist, W.J. Zahnow Elementary School, Waterloo, IL

Paulette Mansell, Certified Reading Recovery Specialist, and Early Literacy Consultant, TX